T0022823

IS YOUR CAT A
PSYCHOPATH?

Copyright © 2022, 2023 by Stephen Wildish
Cover and internal design © 2023 by Sourcebooks

Cover and internal design by Stephen Wildish

Sourcebooks and the colophon are registered trademarks of Sourcebooks.

All rights reserved. No part of this book may be reproduced in any form or by any electronic or mechanical means including information storage and retrieval systems—except in the case of brief quotations embodied in critical articles or reviews—without permission in writing from its publisher, Sourcebooks.

Published by Sourcebooks
P.O. Box 4410, Naperville, Illinois 60567-4410
(630) 961-3900
sourcebooks.com

Originally published in 2022 by Pop Press, an imprint of Ebury Publishing.

Cataloging-in-Publication Data is on file with the Library of Congress.

Printed and bound in the United States of America.
KP 10 9 8 7 6 5 4 3 2 1

IS YOUR CAT A
PSYCHOPATH?

A PERSONALITY QUIZ BOOK to Find Out
If Your Cat Is Pussolini or Mother Purresa

sourcebooks

You don't own a cat.
You own cat food.

CONTENTS

INTRODUCTION

*"Little old me?
Why, I wouldn't
hurt a fly..."*

Cats. We've all met one. The little animals (and sometimes the not-so-little "chonkers") that are covered in fur and smugness and which many people invite into their homes to live. Some people love them and take care of them, some people try to throw them away without a thought.

Have you ever stopped to wonder just who you are inviting in front of your hearth? Is it a cute fluffy animal with a heart full of love or a cold-hearted psychopath with fangs and only killing and hate on their mind? There is a fictional monster that needs inviting in, and which has fangs and loves killing—and that is a vampire. Coincidence? Probably, yes. Vampires don't exist.

This book will help you assess where on the moral axis your cat sits, assign them a comparable personality profile, and give you tips on how to coexist peacefully with your little fur-ball (or dangerous beast), whether they are a psychopath or not.

A CAT

NOT A CAT

ERR...NOT SURE.

First things first, let's just check that you are in fact the owner of a cat and not some other mysterious beast.

This book covers domestic cats and not feral or wild cats. The latter are definitely psychopaths, no question.

If your cat barks, has a waggy tail, and sits on command, you have a dog.

Your cat will be covered in fur, have an air of arrogance, and will meow. Cats are crepuscular (active at dawn and dusk) and have retractable claws and sharp reflexes to the sound of tins of food being opened. Go and check your animal now, then we can proceed.

Is your cat a psychopath?

How have we come to this point in time
when cats are willingly invited into
homes and cared for by humans?
Well, the story starts, as many good
stories do, in Ancient Egypt. OK, some
stories start in Ancient Egypt, I can't name
more than two really *good* stories from
Ancient Egypt, but I'm not an
Egyptologist. I digress.

Archaeologists have discovered that cats
lived independently alongside humans for
thousands of years before they eventually
decided to come in through the door—
presumably only to immediately scratch
at it to be let out again.

Dogs were the first animals to be
domesticated by humans and were bred
specifically for certain jobs and tasks.
This is why the shapes and sizes of dogs
can be as diverse as a sausage dog and a
bloodhound.

"I shall not be tamed! Unless you have tuna;
if you have tuna I might rethink."

———

Unlike dogs, cats chose to be domesticated
and were not going to let us mere humans
tamper with their genetic makeup.

During the process of domestication, cats'
genes have only strayed in minor ways from
those of wildcats; the only real difference is
an apparent settling of temperament and a
tolerance of being around humans.

Is your cat a psychopath?

"Damn thing is covered in glue!"

SHOULD YOU GET ANOTHER CAT?

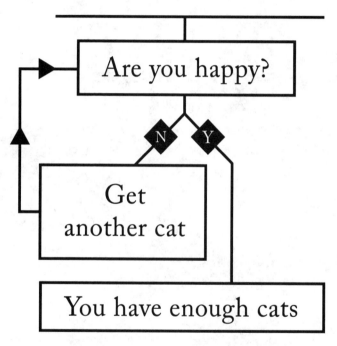

ANCIENT EGYPTIANS WORSHIPPED CATS AS GODS...

...CATS DON'T REALISE THIS IS NO LONGER THE CASE

Is your cat a psychopath?

"Meow to me... I mean, bow to me, peasants!"

Introduction

Although cats were initially useful to have around to keep control of rats and other vermin, drawings and accounts from Ancient Egypt show that cats had somehow persuaded humans to carry them around everywhere rather than having to put their little dainty paws on the dusty floor. Incredible.

In Ancient Egypt cats became gods. Eight of the Egyptian gods were cats, each with their own personality. Here are the top four:

BASTET
Goddess of pleasure. Had an air of disdain and authority.

TEFNUT
Goddess of moisture. Full of wrath, rage, and jealousy. Not an ideal dinner party guest.

SAKHMET
Goddess of war and, confusingly, goddess of healing. Come on, Sakhmet, make your mind up: kill 'em or heal 'em!

PAKHET
Another goddess of war. Her name literally means "she who scratches!"

HOW WELL TRAINED IS YOUR CAT?

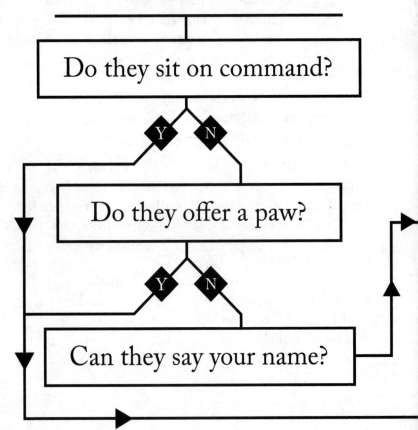

Do they sit on command?

Y N

Do they offer a paw?

Y N

Can they say your name?

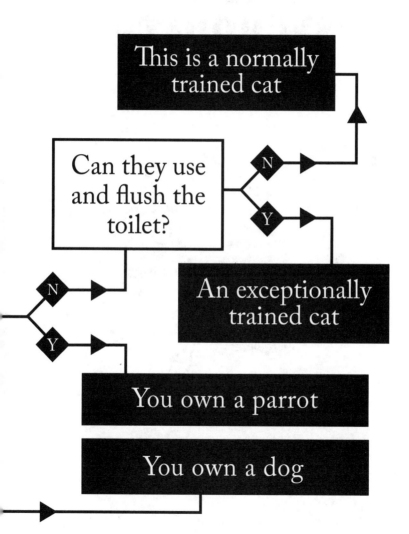

This is a normally trained cat

Can they use and flush the toilet?

N

Y

An exceptionally trained cat

N

Y

You own a parrot

You own a dog

WHAT IS A PSYCHOPATH?

*"RAWR, FLAAARGHW,
MEEEEOOOWW!"*

Before we can establish where on the moral axis your cat sits, and therefore if they are a psychopath or not, we must first ensure that we understand what a psychopath is. Since the early days of worship in the ancient world, cats have become a part of everyday life and a part of most households. In fact, in the US, there are nearly 60 million pet cats, and 25.4 percent of households own at least one cat. That's a figure that is growing each year.

So, that means 60 million potential psychopaths, 60 million scheming little fur-balls, all just biding their time...

"Oh you wait, I will cut you when you sleep."

Is your cat a psychopath?

You may have your suspicions about Tiddles, you may be second-guessing what those cold stares are all about, so to understand if they are a psychopath we must first understand what that is. You're probably full of questions like: "What is the difference between a psychopath and a sociopath?", "Wasn't that Freud guy a psychopath, or am I getting confused with a psychoanalyst?" Well, let me explain, and also, yes, you are getting confused. You're an idiot.

PSYCHOPATHS

When you think of a psychopath, you're probably picturing a stone-cold killer, with an axe, dancing to '80s music, but psychopaths like this are so obvious that they are normally incarcerated pretty quickly. It's the silent types you need to keep an eye out for.

What is a psychopath?

"Bow to me and my shiny boots!"

Is your cat a psychopath?

How many times have you watched the
news after a serial killer has been caught
and in the interviews the neighbours always
say, "He was such a quiet man, you'd never
have guessed he had heads in his fridge,"
missing the point that if he looked like
a murderer you would have guessed and
he wouldn't have committed the murders.
Come on, Sharon, it's not rocket science.

Let's look at some key traits of a
psychopath. First and foremost, and
probably the most important trait, is a
complete and utter absence of a conscience;
they have no remorse whatsoever. This
means psychopaths have an innate inability
to feel no guilt for any of their dastardly
actions.

What is a psychopath?

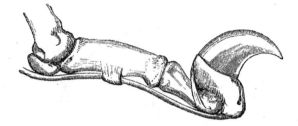

CLAW RETRACTED
Happy cat, purring.

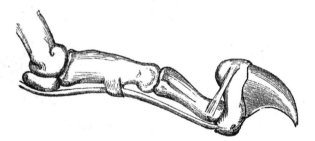

CLAW EXTENDED
Ready for death, seemingly for no
reason on earth.

Is your cat a psychopath?

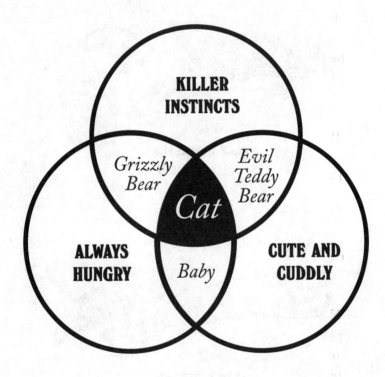

What is a psychopath?

Following on from that trait, and closely linked, are aggression, compulsiveness, and a tendency to be destructive. All of these behaviors coincide with no understanding of others' feelings and little to no regard of the welfare of others.

Psychopaths are easily bored, self-obsessed, and awash with irresponsible impulses. Psychopaths have a habit of finding trouble.

They can be silver-tongued, coldly rational, and highly intelligent, and also happy to exploit the goodwill of others in many ways, but especially financially.

Now go back and read that description of a psychopath again and imagine it's a cat. An ordinary cat. No difference. We can do the test but I think we all know what that little savage is thinking.

"IF CATS COULD TALK, THEY WOULDN'T"

"Err... Meow, I guess?"

Is your cat a psychopath?

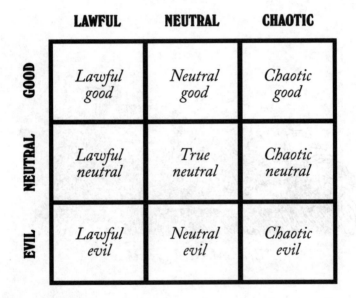

	LAWFUL	**NEUTRAL**	**CHAOTIC**
GOOD	*Lawful good*	*Neutral good*	*Chaotic good*
NEUTRAL	*Lawful neutral*	*True neutral*	*Chaotic neutral*
EVIL	*Lawful evil*	*Neutral evil*	*Chaotic evil*

What is a psychopath?

THE MORAL AXIS

When observing a cat's behavior with a
diagnosis in mind, it's helpful to work out
where the essence of their character fits on
the moral chart opposite.

The easiest way to understand the moral axis
is to imagine the top left square, the lawful
good square, as your *"Goody–Two–shoes"* cat.
This is the cat who is trained to juggle
and can flush the toilet after using it. The
opposing square, the chaotic evil square, is
occupied by an all-out psychopath, a cat
who will sit watching, happily purring,
as you choke to death.

The evil row is where we can possibly find
our psychopaths. Lawful evil is a cat who will
create rules, but their own rules, and then
impose them on your household. The neutral
evil cat doesn't require rules but does evil acts
—and the chaotic evil cat is just a
bloody nightmare.

Is your cat a psychopath?

WAIT, WHAT IS A SOCIOPATH THEN?

"*Sociopath*" and "*psychopath*" are terms that often get mixed up in people's minds, and in some cases they can be used interchangeably, but there are key differences. Psychopaths will have no conscience at all, whereas sociopaths will have a small sprinkling of conscience, a light dusting of morals.

A sociopathic cat might struggle to contain their emotions and will lash out, perhaps with their claws, then later show remorse and ask you for forgiveness with a head boop. A psychopathic cat, on the other hand, may not lash out at all and will certainly not offer a peace lily or a furry paw of apology.

Sociopathic cats care about things, sometimes too much, while psychopaths pretend to care but inside is a cold, cold fluffy heart. Both might claw you to death but only one will care about it later.

What is a psychopath?

"I'm so ashamed."

Is your cat a psychopath?

*"I thought I was wrong once,
but I was mistaken."*

What is a psychopath?

BUT WHY SO SUPERIOR?

You only have to have seen a cat once to
know that they carry an air of superiority
over all they meet. But why is this, and is it
a characteristic of a psychopath?

Cats believe that their abilities—both mental
and physical—are far greater than they are. In
many ways they are highly skilled—at walking
on fences, making vast jumps, and training
humans to clear their poo away and feed them
on demand. But they are, of course, flawed:
we've all seen a cat miss a jump or fall off the
corner of a chair, clawing desperately to get
back up. They are flawed, but they are arrogant
enough to refuse to accept it.

Is this arrogance and superiority a symptom
of an underlying psychopathy? Possibly;
the lack of humility required to be quite so
breathtakingly arrogant is certainly a red flag.

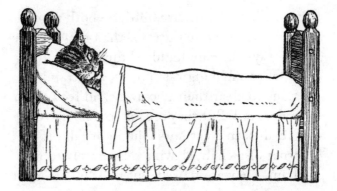

"Try me."

SHOULD YOU WAKE UP YOUR CAT?

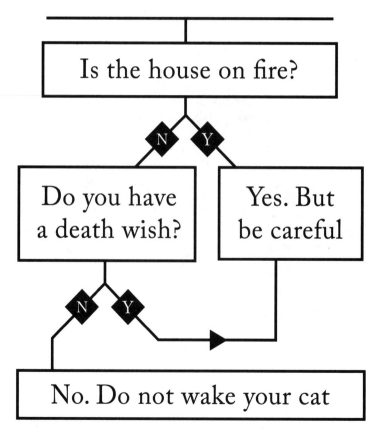

UNUSUAL CAT BEHAVIORS

"Delicious slops!"

The following behaviors, while weird and wonderful, are often tell tale signs of a psychopath. Should you witness these, you should be on your guard...

GETTING THE ZOOMIES

Younger cats and kittens are hugely playful and energetic, and sometimes this energy can boil over into a running frenzy in your front room, smashing into furniture and knocking over ornaments with seemingly no regard for their own safety or your possessions. If you find yourself with a cat dangling from the lampshade, this could be a sign of psychopathy.

Energy frenzies like this can also be brought on by catnip, in which case, if this is anyone's fault, it's yours.

SLEEPING IN WEIRD PLACES

You'd be a fool to think that cats sleeping in the weirdest of places is about comfort. This is about knowing the exits and dominating your space. Yes, that empty box is theirs and they definitely need to take possession of the clean washing pile.

"If I fits, I sits."

HEAD BOOPING

Cats love a head boop, and we've all been led to believe that it's cat language for "I love you." But what if this is just them lulling you into a false sense of security? Some experts believe that this is actually a sign of the cat marking you with their scent. They're really saying "I love you" in an "I own you" kind of way.

WEIRD MEOWING

Cats not only meow, they can chirp, yowl, hack, and chatter. These strange noises can be especially disconcerting in the middle of the night and the early hours, when, aside from it being a plea for attention, it could also be a form of psychological torture designed to test just how far they can push you before you break. Meeeooooowww!

Is your cat a psychopath?

"I've seen things."

STARING INTO SPACE

There are a few reasons why cats
seemingly stare into space:

1. They've had too much catnip and
are completely and utterly stoned.

2. They are watching something you can't
see. Cats' vision is far superior to that of
us humans and they are able to see even
tiny bugs from a distance.

3. There is a ghost in your house and it has
a warning about the future that only the
cats can see.

Unusual cat behaviors

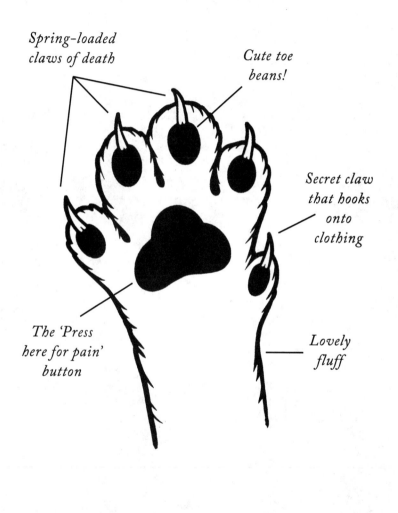

Spring-loaded claws of death

Cute toe beans!

Secret claw that hooks onto clothing

The 'Press here for pain' button

Lovely fluff

"I WISH I COULD WRITE AS MYSTERIOUS AS A CAT"

Edgar Allen Poe, mystery writer

"I'm a real riddle, but get me a saucer of milk and I will tell all!"

Is your cat a psychopath?

BRINGING HOME BODY PARTS

Are you even a cat owner if at some point you haven't been surprised by the gift of a bloody cadaver of a mouse or garden bird?

Cats take great pleasure in killing small animals, they absolutely love it. Although some people want to believe that this is a "gift" or a misguided sign of love, this is about making you an accomplice in their murders. Or perhaps it is reminding you that you could be next—you've seen that scene in *The Godfather*, right?

The only real cure for this behavior is to keep your cat inside and literally away from the pigeons...mice, newts, and shrews.

*"Yes, yes, you will make a
fitting present for master."*

Is your cat a psychopath?

KNEADING YOU
Cats who knead are nothing to be concerned about. Young kittens knead their mothers to stimulate milk production. When an adult cat kneads you in this way it is a bit like a toddler sucking their thumb. It is a behavior that makes them feel relaxed and content. They could of course be employing a different tactic altogether—probing you for weak spots to find the best attack points.

KNOCKING THINGS OFF SURFACES
Cats do tend to enjoy knocking all sorts of items—pens, glasses, Ming vases, etc.—off tables and shelves. But why? Are they trying to get your attention or do they know exactly what they are doing, wearing you down with a form of slow torture?

DRINKING FROM THE TAP
Cats do this because the water you have placed down for them is simply not good enough for their precious little mouths.

*"I hold respect for none
of your foolish rules, human."*

"WHAT GREATER GIFT THAN THE LOVE OF A CAT"

Serial adulterer and terrible
father Charles Dickens

"I'm an awful turd."

Dickens's beloved cat Bob died in 1862. And like a bit of a maniac, Dickens had its paw stuffed and made into an ivory-handled letter opener.

If only Charles had loved his wife and ten children as much as Bob. Much like a psychopath himself, Dickens was saintly in public and a cruel man in private. In 1858, after twenty-two years of marriage, he claimed his wife was mad and tried to have her institutionalized so he could marry a younger woman.

Is your cat a psychopath?

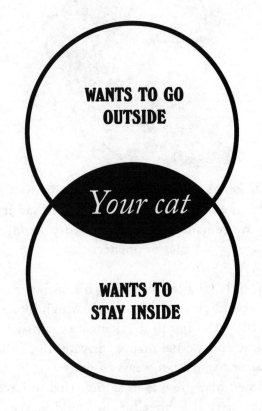

WANTS TO GO
OUTSIDE

Your cat

WANTS TO
STAY INSIDE

INDECISIVENESS

Most cats will exhibit indecisive behavior, such as going out and then instantly wanting to come back in again, exploring a box and backing out in seconds, hissing and then purring within minutes of each other. Their emotions can turn on a dime. Are they really this indecisive or are they toying with us?

Some cats seem to be highly inquisitive but also timid, so it could be this mix of wanting to explore/make decisions and being scared that these decisions will lead to a catastrophe (pun entirely intended) that makes our frustrating felines change their minds so often. That's not to say that some cats don't enjoy the fun game of making you do things for them. You can see the smirk on their cute little faces.

Is your cat a psychopath?

Most cats will exhibit a few unusual quirks around eating. These might include:

GORGING
Gorging might be down to how your cat is being fed—for example, are there other cats around that might compete for the food? Do you feed them one large meal each day? Consider serving smaller portions throughout the day, but don't be alarmed when your cat judges you for having double dessert after your mammoth evening feast.

ONLY EATING ALONE
Cats prefer to eat alone, in a calm environment away from any potential, larger "predators." Genuine question, have you tried to eat their food at some point?

PLAYING WITH FOOD
This is just cats' predatory instincts kicking in. They're hunting, albeit incredibly badly, their kibble.

WILL YOUR CAT EAT YOU?

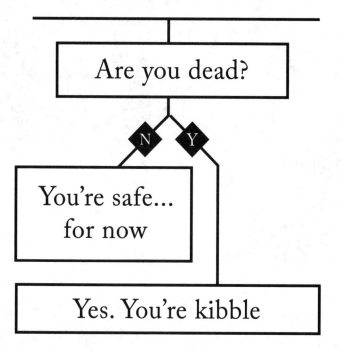

"DIXIE IS SMARTER THAN MY WHOLE CABINET"

Abraham Lincoln, talking about his pet cat Dixie

Unusual cat behaviors

As well as being the inventor of the chin strap beard, Lincoln was a complete cat lover! Lincoln doted on his two cats, Dixie and Tabby. So much so, in fact, that he once fed Tabby at the table during a formal dinner.

Those are two cats that had a miraculous hold over a powerful man. They essentially held the reins of power over an entire nation. Clever cats.

DOES YOUR CAT LOVE YOU?

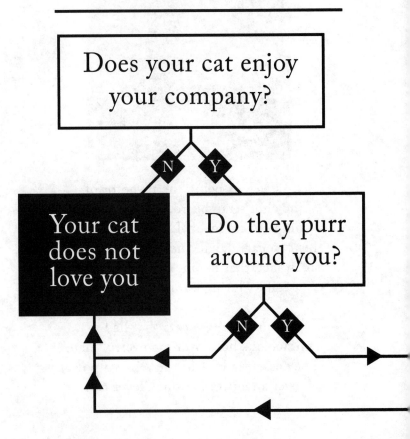

Does your cat enjoy your company?

N / Y

Your cat does not love you

Do they purr around you?

N / Y

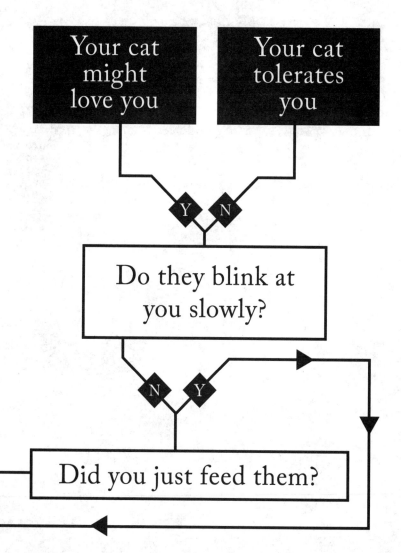

Your cat might love you

Your cat tolerates you

Y   N

Do they blink at you slowly?

N   Y

Did you just feed them?

"OH WUZZA SCHUCKUMS PSST, PSST, WHO'S A LOVELY BOY THEN?"

Catherine the Great
(Probably)

Unusual cat behaviors

Catherine the Great was the OG cat lady. She loved cats so much that she had not one but two gangs of cats operating at her Winter Palace in St. Petersburg. She kept a large group of elegant Russian blues on the upper floors of the palace, with free-roaming rights. They were obviously pampered beyond belief.

Kept in the basement was an army of "working" cats, trained to hunt and kill rodents. In a classic cat lady move, Catherine officially promoted these cats to palace guards, complete with wages and benefits.

THE QUESTIONNAIRE

*"I'm biding my sweet time,
you little morsels of food."*

The questionnaire

This list of forty questions asks you to rank your cat's behaviors from 1 (no way!) to 5 (very much so) in certain situations to evaluate four key areas of their character: Bold or Wary, Sociable or Unsociable, Crazy or Restrained, and Mean or Nice. The scoring will give your cat a value for each of these qualities: B for bold, U for Unsociable, C for Crazy, and N for Nice, for example.

BOLD VS WARY

Is your cat overly brave, seemingly without fear? Perhaps they often scrap with neighbours' cats or love nothing more than going off on a far-flung hunting expedition?

SOCIABLE VS UNSOCIABLE

Does your cat much prefer alone time? Do they actively avoid humans and other pets? Well, when they are not attacking them.

Is your cat a psychopath?

CRAZY VS RESTRAINED
Does your cat exhibit impulsive
behavior, scatty-ness, and a general
unawareness of their surroundings.
They can't plan to save their life and are
oblivious to the fact that their actions have
consequences. Is this genuine behavior or
are they just seeking attention?

MEAN VS NICE
Fairly straightforward, is your cat a little
bastard? Aggressive, spiteful, and happy to
defecate/urinate anywhere? Oh dear.

So let's find out if your cat is indeed a
hateful Hannibal Lickter waiting to strike,
or a budding Dolly Purrton waiting to dazzle.

SECTION 1: BOLDNESS

QUESTION 1

My cat can be found in silly and often dangerous places where they should not be.

5	4	3	2	1
VERY MUCH SO	**YES, I GUESS**	**NOT SURE**	**NOT REALLY**	**NO WAY!**
○	○	○	○	○

QUESTION 2

If we had a new shed my cat would be the first in it, knocking things over and being a nuisance.

5	4	3	2	1
VERY MUCH SO	**YES, I GUESS**	**NOT SURE**	**NOT REALLY**	**NO WAY!**
○	○	○	○	○

Is your cat a psychopath?

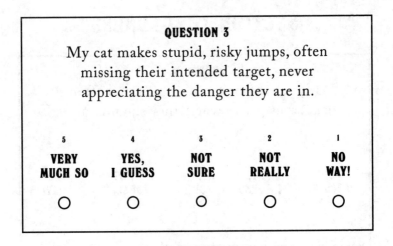

QUESTION 3

My cat makes stupid, risky jumps, often missing their intended target, never appreciating the danger they are in.

5	4	3	2	1
VERY MUCH SO	**YES, I GUESS**	**NOT SURE**	**NOT REALLY**	**NO WAY!**
○	○	○	○	○

QUESTION 4

My cat climbs trees, big stupid trees.

5	4	3	2	1
VERY MUCH SO	**YES, I GUESS**	**NOT SURE**	**NOT REALLY**	**NO WAY!**
○	○	○	○	○

QUESTION 5

My cat sits on the top of the sofa,
judging us all.

5	4	3	2	1
VERY MUCH SO	**YES, I GUESS**	**NOT SURE**	**NOT REALLY**	**NO WAY!**
O	O	O	O	O

QUESTION 6

Other cats will NOT
be tolerated in "their garden."

5	4	3	2	1
VERY MUCH SO	**YES, I GUESS**	**NOT SURE**	**NOT REALLY**	**NO WAY!**
O	O	O	O	O

Is your cat a psychopath?

QUESTION 7
If my cat could pack a knapsack and go wandering, they would, and they would be gone for days.

5	4	3	2	1
VERY MUCH SO	**YES, I GUESS**	**NOT SURE**	**NOT REALLY**	**NO WAY!**
○	○	○	○	○

QUESTION 8
My cat sometimes behaves like a dog. Woof woof, meow meow.

5	4	3	2	1
VERY MUCH SO	**YES, I GUESS**	**NOT SURE**	**NOT REALLY**	**NO WAY!**
○	○	○	○	○

QUESTION 9

My cat struts around the house
like the Queen of Sheba.

5	4	3	2	1
VERY MUCH SO	**YES, I GUESS**	**NOT SURE**	**NOT REALLY**	**NO WAY!**
○	○	○	○	○

QUESTION 10

My cat seems to be operating a mob
protection racket in the area, regularly
fighting other cats.

5	4	3	2	1
VERY MUCH SO	**YES, I GUESS**	**NOT SURE**	**NOT REALLY**	**NO WAY!**
○	○	○	○	○

BOLDNESS SCORE:

SECTION 2: SOCIABILITY

QUESTION 11

My cat often seems bored and craves stimulation, especially when I am on a Zoom call.

5	4	3	2	1
VERY MUCH SO	YES, I GUESS	NOT SURE	NOT REALLY	NO WAY!
○	○	○	○	○

QUESTION 12

My house can be filled with meows, yowls, or screeches for no bloody reason.

5	4	3	2	1
VERY MUCH SO	YES, I GUESS	NOT SURE	NOT REALLY	NO WAY!
○	○	○	○	○

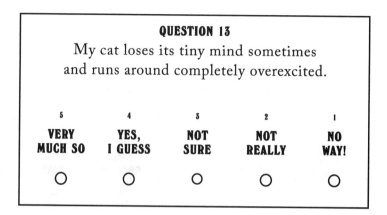

QUESTION 13

My cat loses its tiny mind sometimes
and runs around completely overexcited.

5	4	3	2	1
VERY MUCH SO	YES, I GUESS	NOT SURE	NOT REALLY	NO WAY!
○	○	○	○	○

QUESTION 14

My cat demands strokes and will
not leave me alone until I am
giving it attention.

5	4	3	2	1
VERY MUCH SO	YES, I GUESS	NOT SURE	NOT REALLY	NO WAY!
○	○	○	○	○

Is your cat a psychopath?

QUESTION 15
My laptop apparently makes an excellent
seat for my cat and that is probably why
I own it. So they can sit on it.

5	4	3	2	1
VERY MUCH SO	YES, I GUESS	NOT SURE	NOT REALLY	NO WAY!
O	O	O	O	O

QUESTION 16
The house is sometimes
treated like a racetrack for cats.

5	4	3	2	1
VERY MUCH SO	YES, I GUESS	NOT SURE	NOT REALLY	NO WAY!
O	O	O	O	O

"Don't mind me, just wiping this mud off."

Is your cat a psychopath?

QUESTION 17
My cat will follow
me around meowing.

5	4	3	2	1
VERY MUCH SO	YES, I GUESS	NOT SURE	NOT REALLY	NO WAY!
○	○	○	○	○

QUESTION 18
My cat loves being around me and
will even move from a comfy bed
to snuggle up.

5	4	3	2	1
VERY MUCH SO	YES, I GUESS	NOT SURE	NOT REALLY	NO WAY!
○	○	○	○	○

QUESTION 19
My cat pesters people
using meowing and paws.

5	4	3	2	1
VERY MUCH SO	**YES, I GUESS**	**NOT SURE**	**NOT REALLY**	**NO WAY!**
○	○	○	○	○

QUESTION 20
My cat is easily distracted and will stare
at things that appear to be nothing.

5	4	3	2	1
VERY MUCH SO	**YES, I GUESS**	**NOT SURE**	**NOT REALLY**	**NO WAY!**
○	○	○	○	○

SOCIABILITY SCORE:

SECTION 3: CRAZINESS

QUESTION 21

My cat is a little idiot, always getting
themselves into scrapes.
Danger is their middle name!

5	4	3	2	1
VERY MUCH SO	**YES, I GUESS**	**NOT SURE**	**NOT REALLY**	**NO WAY!**
○	○	○	○	○

QUESTION 22

My cat always does things I don't want them
to do. They know it, but they don't care.

5	4	3	2	1
VERY MUCH SO	**YES, I GUESS**	**NOT SURE**	**NOT REALLY**	**NO WAY!**
○	○	○	○	○

QUESTION 23

My cat has been known to steal food from my plate and drink from my glass. Apparently we share everything.

5	4	3	2	1
VERY MUCH SO	**YES, I GUESS**	**NOT SURE**	**NOT REALLY**	**NO WAY!**
○	○	○	○	○

QUESTION 24

My cat is a pouncer, hiding and pouncing on me as I pass like I am a mouse.

5	4	3	2	1
VERY MUCH SO	**YES, I GUESS**	**NOT SURE**	**NOT REALLY**	**NO WAY!**
○	○	○	○	○

Is your cat a psychopath?

QUESTION 25

My cat doesn't react if
I shout or punish them.

5	4	3	2	1
VERY MUCH SO	**YES, I GUESS**	**NOT SURE**	**NOT REALLY**	**NO WAY!**
○	○	○	○	○

QUESTION 26

My cat pushes things off shelves and
stares at me while they do it. The more
expensive the item, the better.

5	4	3	2	1
VERY MUCH SO	**YES, I GUESS**	**NOT SURE**	**NOT REALLY**	**NO WAY!**
○	○	○	○	○

The questionnaire

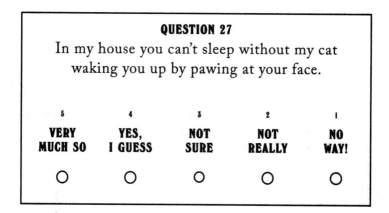

QUESTION 27

In my house you can't sleep without my cat
waking you up by pawing at your face.

5	4	3	2	1
VERY MUCH SO	**YES, I GUESS**	**NOT SURE**	**NOT REALLY**	**NO WAY!**
O	O	O	O	O

QUESTION 28

My cat is vicious during play,
the claws are always out.

5	4	3	2	1
VERY MUCH SO	**YES, I GUESS**	**NOT SURE**	**NOT REALLY**	**NO WAY!**
O	O	O	O	O

Is your cat a psychopath?

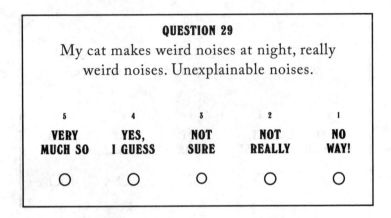

QUESTION 29

My cat makes weird noises at night, really weird noises. Unexplainable noises.

5	4	3	2	1
VERY MUCH SO	**YES, I GUESS**	**NOT SURE**	**NOT REALLY**	**NO WAY!**
○	○	○	○	○

QUESTION 30

I don't think my cat cares if they have done something bad. No remorse.

5	4	3	2	1
VERY MUCH SO	**YES, I GUESS**	**NOT SURE**	**NOT REALLY**	**NO WAY!**
○	○	○	○	○

CRAZINESS SCORE:

"I've brought you a gift, a terrifying gift."

SECTION 4: MEANNESS

QUESTION 31
My cat has people they definitely do not like. They will show them their displeasure.

5	4	3	2	1
VERY MUCH SO	**YES, I GUESS**	**NOT SURE**	**NOT REALLY**	**NO WAY!**
○	○	○	○	○

QUESTION 32
My cat is the top cat.
They boss around other cats.

5	4	3	2	1
VERY MUCH SO	**YES, I GUESS**	**NOT SURE**	**NOT REALLY**	**NO WAY!**
○	○	○	○	○

QUESTION 33

Other cats are scared of my bruiser
of a cat. What they think is play is
often too rough.

5	4	3	2	1
VERY MUCH SO	**YES, I GUESS**	**NOT SURE**	**NOT REALLY**	**NO WAY!**
◯	◯	◯	◯	◯

QUESTION 34

My cat makes other cats move for them,
even if the other cat is asleep.

5	4	3	2	1
VERY MUCH SO	**YES, I GUESS**	**NOT SURE**	**NOT REALLY**	**NO WAY!**
◯	◯	◯	◯	◯

Is your cat a psychopath?

QUESTION 35
Embarrassingly, my cat
is in charge of me.

5	4	3	2	1
VERY MUCH SO	**YES, I GUESS**	**NOT SURE**	**NOT REALLY**	**NO WAY!**
O	O	O	O	O

QUESTION 36
You do NOT pet my cat;
they are not here for strokes.

5	4	3	2	1
VERY MUCH SO	**YES, I GUESS**	**NOT SURE**	**NOT REALLY**	**NO WAY!**
O	O	O	O	O

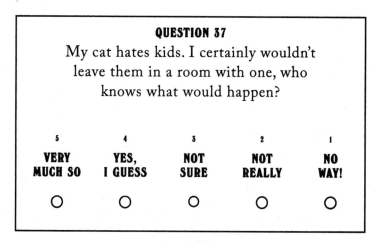

QUESTION 37

My cat hates kids. I certainly wouldn't leave them in a room with one, who knows what would happen?

5	4	3	2	1
VERY MUCH SO	**YES, I GUESS**	**NOT SURE**	**NOT REALLY**	**NO WAY!**
○	○	○	○	○

QUESTION 38

My cat can take an instant dislike to someone and be horrible to them.

5	4	3	2	1
VERY MUCH SO	**YES, I GUESS**	**NOT SURE**	**NOT REALLY**	**NO WAY!**
○	○	○	○	○

Is your cat a psychopath?

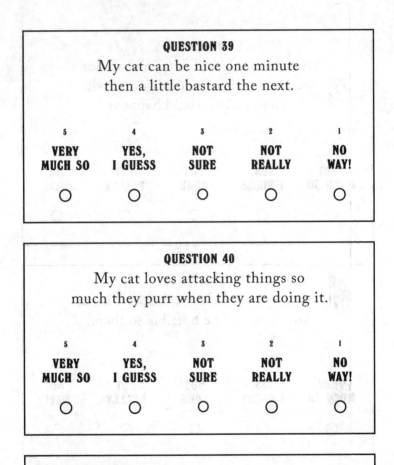

QUESTION 39
My cat can be nice one minute
then a little bastard the next.

5	4	3	2	1
VERY MUCH SO	**YES, I GUESS**	**NOT SURE**	**NOT REALLY**	**NO WAY!**
○	○	○	○	○

QUESTION 40
My cat loves attacking things so
much they purr when they are doing it.

5	4	3	2	1
VERY MUCH SO	**YES, I GUESS**	**NOT SURE**	**NOT REALLY**	**NO WAY!**
○	○	○	○	○

MEANNESS SCORE:

"We're playing a fun game!"

Is your cat a psychopath?

That's it, you're done! Time to add
up your scores and let's see what
purrsonality your cat has.

Questions 1—10

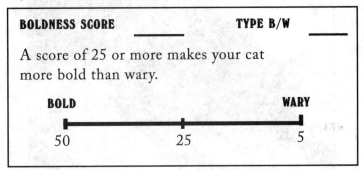

BOLDNESS SCORE _____   **TYPE B/W** _____

A score of 25 or more makes your cat
more bold than wary.

BOLD   **WARY**

50   25   5

Questions 11—20

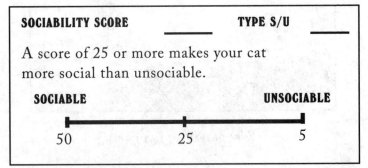

SOCIABILITY SCORE _____   **TYPE S/U** _____

A score of 25 or more makes your cat
more social than unsociable.

SOCIABLE   **UNSOCIABLE**

50   25   5

The questionnaire

Questions 21—30

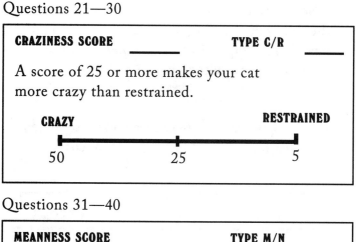

CRAZINESS SCORE _____   **TYPE C/R** _____

A score of 25 or more makes your cat more crazy than restrained.

CRAZY   **RESTRAINED**

50   25   5

Questions 31—40

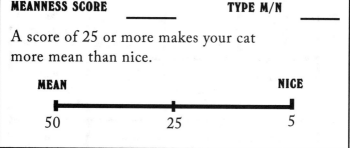

MEANNESS SCORE _____   **TYPE M/N** _____

A score of 25 or more makes your cat more mean than nice.

MEAN   **NICE**

50   25   5

Is your cat a psychopath?

Now you have your cat's score, we can place the four values together to make a purrsonality type. For example, *Wary, Unsociable, Restrained,* and *Mean* come together to make the type: **WURM.**

On the opposite page we can see how these sixteen types each correspond to a different cat character.

		WARY		BOLD	
		UNSOCIABLE	SOCIABLE	UNSOCIABLE	
RESTRAINED	MEAN	*Wary, unsociable, restrained, mean*	*Wary, sociable, restrained, mean*	*Bold, sociable, restrained, mean*	*Bold, unsociable, restrained, mean*
	NICE	*Wary, unsociable, restrained, nice*	*Wary, sociable, restrained, nice*	*Bold, sociable, restrained, nice*	*Bold unsociable, restrained, nice*
CRAZY	NICE	*Wary, unsociable, crazy, nice*	*Wary, sociable, crazy, nice*	*Bold, sociable, crazy, nice*	*Bold, unsociable, crazy, nice*
	MEAN	*Wary, unsociable, crazy, mean*	*Wary, sociable, crazy, mean*	*Bold, sociable, crazy, mean*	*Bold unsociable, crazy, mean*

Purrsonality types

WURM *Mark Zucker-furred* *Page 94*	**WSRM** *Margaret Catcher* *Page 96*	**BSRM** *Pawdon Ramsay* *Page 98*	**BURM** *Winston Furchill* *Page 100*
WURN *Meow-hatma Gandhi* *Page 102*	**WSRN** *Catbed Sheeran* *Page 104*	**BSRN** *Leonardo DiCatrio* *Page 106*	**BURN** *Mother Purresa* *Page 108*
WUCN *Pablo Purrcasso* *Page 110*	**WSCN** *Meow-chelle Obama* *Page 112*	**BSCN** *Dolly Purrton* *Page 114*	**BUCN** *Purrlock Holmes* *Page 116*
WUCM *Napawleon Bone-a-purrte* *Page 118*	**WSCM** *Hannibal Lickter* *Page 120*	**BSCM** *Clawo-patra* *Page 122*	**BUCM** *Pussolini* *Page 124*

"YOU'VE CAT TO BE KITTEN ME RIGHT MEOW"

Humorous T-shirt

"Ha-bloody-ha!"

WURM

MARK ZUCKER-FURRED

"My precious!"

KEY PURRSONALITY TYPE
Mark Zucker-furred is Wary, Unsociable,
Restrained, and Mean. A real character,
but not one you might want to know.

BEHAVIORS TO WATCH OUT FOR
They very much know their own minds,
will not be coaxed into performing tricks,
and should never, ever be awoken from
a sleep. Feed them their favourite food,
exactly when they require it, or they might
cut you when you sleep with one of those
sharpened claws they keep.

TIPS ON PEACEFUL COEXISTENCE
Mark gets on well with no one. He doesn't
like anyone. Good luck.

PSYCHOPATH VERDICT
Not a psychopath, just really
unfriendly. I'm sure they have some
loveable features. Possibly?

Is your cat a psychopath?

"*This feline is not for turning!*"

KEY PURRSONALITY TYPE
Margaret Catcher is Wary, Sociable, Restrained, and Mean. She will snatch your milk but charm you while she does it.

BEHAVIORS TO WATCH OUT FOR
Margaret Catcher will steal your food when you're not looking, meow to be let out and then remember that she doesn't like being outside, and stare at the open door wondering why you opened it. You should know she would do this, this is on you.

TIPS ON PEACEFUL COEXISTENCE
Can be hard work to please. Keep her well fed and comfy and you should be well respected.

PSYCHOPATH VERDICT
Possible psychopath. The ability to be sociable and mean at the same time shows little empathy, but maybe there is some left in that cold heart of theirs.

Is your cat a psychopath?

BSRM

PAWDON
RAMSAY

"Are you an idiot sandwich?"

KEY PURRSONALITY TYPE

Pawdon Ramsay is Bold, Sociable, Restrained, and Mean. He will take uncalculated risks and exhibit rash behavior. He is reserved with his feelings and is known to lash out at others if their behavior doesn't suit him.

BEHAVIORS TO LOOK OUT FOR

Pawdon will meow if he's not getting enough attention. He will also judge his dinner and turn his nose up if you've overcooked the fish.

TIPS ON PEACEFUL COEXISTENCE

Pawdon gets on well with most cats and people, his mean streak only comes out when provoked.

PSYCHOPATH VERDICT

Not a psychopath, his overriding boldness and sociable character make Pawdon a good cat to have around.

"I'm no bulldog!"

KEY PURRSONALITY TYPE
Winston is Bold, Unsociable,
Restrained, and Mean.
Winston very much rules the roost.

BEHAVIORS TO WATCH OUT FOR
He also enjoys order and having
everything to his liking. Try to introduce
a new routine and Winston will stand his
ground. He will fight you in the bedrooms,
he will fight you on the landing.

TIPS ON PEACEFUL COEXISTENCE
Keep regular mealtimes, offer strokes
when required, and leave them to it.

PSYCHOPATH VERDICT
Not a psychopath, Winston believes he is
keeping the house in order for the greater
good. But sometimes he's not pleasant to
be around. A very divisive cat.

Is your cat a psychopath?

"*Mew.*"

KEY PURRSONALITY TYPE

Meow-hatma is Wary, Unsociable, Restrained, and Nice. When he is around he can be loveable and affectionate but equally he can hide in a cupboard, box, or other unusual receptacle.

BEHAVIORS TO WATCH OUT FOR

Meow-hatma loves to keep himself to himself and can even be described as a recluse. It may even feel like sometimes you don't own a cat as they can be in hiding most of the day.

TIPS ON PEACEFUL COEXISTENCE

Try to coax Meow-hatma out of his shell with some special treats.

PSYCHOPATH VERDICT

Not a psychopath, Meow-hatma is reserved and level headed.

Is your cat a psychopath?

WSRN

CATBED
SHEERAN

"Let's have a singsong around the bins."

KEY PURRSONALITY TYPE

Catbed is Wary, Sociable, Restrained, and Nice. You have to earn his trust, but when you do he will be a soppy mess, fawning at your feet and following you around like a lost puppy.

BEHAVIORS TO WATCH OUT FOR

Catbed can love too much; he can become clingy and needy. Let's hope he doesn't learn how to play the acoustic guitar or he would be meowing you love songs at 3 a.m.

TIPS ON PEACEFUL COEXISTENCE

Life with Catbed Sheeran is pretty peaceful already. Introducing another cat into the house might not go down so well, as Catbed is prone to bouts of jealousy.

PSYCHOPATH VERDICT

Not a psychopath, Catbed Sheeran is full of empathy; if anything he feels too much. Tone it down a bit, Catbed. Tone it down.

Is your cat a psychopath?

BSRN

LEONARDO DiCATRIO

"You poor simple fools, more treats!"

KEY PURRSONALITY TYPE

Leo is Bold, Sociable, Restrained, and Nice.
A charming cat loved up and down the street.

BEHAVIORS TO WATCH OUT FOR

Leonardo will be pushing his charms all over.
He can be found acting like nobody feeds him
for payment in treats in multiple houses and
getting pets from everyone he meets.

TIPS ON PEACEFUL COEXISTENCE

Keeping Leonardo tied down to one owner can
prove difficult. There is a danger that some
of his regular stops on the street might start
posting on Facebook about the local uncared-
for cat that nobody owns. When in reality the
greedy pig is having double dinners!

PSYCHOPATH VERDICT

Possible psychopath, surely no one
can be that nice?

Is your cat a psychopath?

BURN

MOTHER PURRESA

"Peace begins with a meow."

KEY PURRSONALITY TYPE

Mother Purresa is Bold, Unsociable, Restrained, and Nice. Overall a pleasant cat who lives frugally and at a somewhat leisurely pace. Why waste energy on walking when sitting and watching will do? Mother Purresa is not entirely bothered with food, she will take or leave it seemingly on a whim.

BEHAVIORS TO WATCH OUT FOR

Although she is restrained, her bold streak means Mother Purresa knows her own mind and will be stubborn, sometimes lashing out if things don't go the way she wants them to.

TIPS ON PEACEFUL COEXISTENCE

Left to her own devices Mother Purresa will do nothing all day and not interact with you at all. She needs gentle coaxing with play, and new and flavorsome treats regularly.

PSYCHOPATH VERDICT

Not a psychopath, a quiet, simple-living cat.

Is your cat a psychopath?

WUCN

PABLO PURRCASSO

"Every cat is an artist."

KEY PURRSONALITY TYPE

Pablo is Wary, Unsociable, Crazy, and Nice. He has a creative flair all of his own; he sees things that aren't there. Maybe he can see ghosts? He is pretty scatty so he will be making crashing and bashing noises at 3 a.m., leaving you to believe that you do in fact have a poltergeist.

BEHAVIORS TO WATCH OUT FOR

Pablo likes to be alone, to create. His crazy nature gets him into trouble when exploring neighbours' houses. He knows no boundaries. If that means he eats all the food from the cat two doors down, then so be it.

TIPS ON PEACEFUL COEXISTENCE

Keeping Pablo from decorating the kitchen floor with mouse and bird innards can be a challenge.

PSYCHOPATH VERDICT

Not a psychopath, just a bit crazy.

Is your cat a psychopath?

"I'm very becoming."

KEY PURRSONALITY TYPE

Meow-chelle is Wary, Sociable, Crazy, and Nice. She is almost the purrfect cat to have around.

BEHAVIORS TO WATCH OUT FOR

Bouts of crazy behavior mean Meow-chelle can be unpredictable, but you can't stay mad at such a friendly and nice cat. Look at that face; butter wouldn't melt.

TIPS ON PEACEFUL COEXISTENCE

Be wary of who Meow-chelle invites into the house to play. Some of her chums from the street will not be quite as nice as her.

PSYCHOPATH VERDICT

Not a psychopath, far from it.

Is your cat a psychopath?

"Meowing nine to five."

KEY PURRSONALITY TYPE
Dolly Purrton is Bold, Sociable, Crazy, and Nice. She will make herself known to all visitors with some extremely scatty behavior.

BEHAVIORS TO WATCH OUT FOR
Dolly loves to sing, and by that I mean she loves to meow outside doors and windows for no reason, day or night. This can become a problem if you like sleeping.

TIPS ON PEACEFUL COEXISTENCE
Take your priceless Ming vases off the shelves. Dolly loves to cause a bit of chaos, so they will be smashed in no time if left.

PSYCHOPATH VERDICT
Not a psychopath; crazy, but not a psychopath.

Is your cat a psychopath?

BUCN

PURRLOCK HOLMES

"Elementary!"

KEY PURRSONALITY TYPE

Purrlock Holmes is Bold, Unsociable, Crazy, and Nice. He is a wise old owl, but not an owl—a cat. Obviously. If Purrlock could play chess he would beat you in three moves, but he'd try to make you feel better about it. He doesn't gloat.

BEHAVIORS TO WATCH OUT FOR

Purrlock has a superiority complex. He assumes he owns the house and everything in it, including you. He cares for his "possessions," so you are not in any danger.

TIPS ON PEACEFUL COEXISTENCE

Let Purrlock live his life as the boss. We know the reality...or do we? Is he actually in charge of all of us?

PSYCHOPATH VERDICT

Borderline psychopath, Purrlock's superior intelligence and crazy instincts mean he doesn't understand your puny emotions but he knows right from wrong.

Is your cat a psychopath?

WUCM

NAPAWLEON BONE-A-PURRTE

"I shall conquer the living room."

KEY PURRSONALITY TYPE

Napawleon is Wary, Unsociable, Crazy, and Mean. In many ways he shares a purrsonality with Purrlock Holmes, but crucially, where Purrlock is nice, Napawleon is mean. Napawleon spends many hours plotting. Nobody knows what he's plotting but it's probably not a lovely birthday surprise.

BEHAVIORS TO WATCH OUT FOR

He will stop at nothing short of global domination, or at the very least domination of the living room.

TIPS ON PEACEFUL COEXISTENCE

Buy yourself a tricorn hat and eye-patch for the inevitable Battle of Waterloo that will take place in the kitchen.

PSYCHOPATH VERDICT

A megalomaniac with no understanding of right and wrong? Yes, he's a psychopath.

Is your cat a psychopath?

WSCM

HANNIBAL LICKTER

"I'll eat this kibble with some fava beans and a nice chianti."

KEY PURRSONALITY TYPE

Hannibal Lickter is Wary, Sociable, Crazy, and Mean. His sociable nature means he enjoys being around humans. His sniffs and licks might be affection, or they might just be tasting the fresh meat.

BEHAVIORS TO WATCH OUT FOR

Murdering you in your sleep. Seriously, those claws are being kept sharp for a purpose.

TIPS ON PEACEFUL COEXISTENCE

Their lust for blood means a constant parade of small animal cadavers on the doormat. Keep wet wipes and a special bin handy.

PSYCHOPATH VERDICT

Psychopath, but at least you know he's one. He's certainly not a hidden psychopath.

"*I am the queen!*"

KEY PURRSONALITY TYPE
The Clawopatra cat is Bold, Sociable, Crazy, and Mean. Clawopatra is extremely judgemental, nothing is good enough for her.

BEHAVIORS TO LOOK OUT FOR
She loves to sit on high, on her throne, and judge you. She leads the pack, but she does love her subjects, just not as much as herself.

TIPS ON PEACEFUL COEXISTENCE
Clawopatra gets on well with any cat or person that doesn't mind being dominated. So let her have her way.

PSYCHOPATH VERDICT
Not a psychopath, she has a shred of empathy, but she is a bit too big for her boots.

Is your cat a psychopath?

"*I require war, unless it's dinner time.*"

KEY PURRSONALITY TYPE
Pussolini is Bold, Unsociable, Crazy, and Mean. His boldness is a key characteristic of his type. He is scared of nothing and wants worship from all around him. He also loves to eat. If cats had banquets, he would be at the head of the table, eating chicken legs Henry-the-Eighth-style.

BEHAVIORS TO WATCH OUT FOR
He is also incredibly stupid, as dumb as a fencepost. He is constantly getting stuck up trees or knocking over large objects with his larger frame.

TIPS ON PEACEFUL COEXISTENCE
Because he's ruled by his belly, Pussolini is fairly easy to manage and to keep tame. The right treats will do the trick.

PSYCHOPATH VERDICT
Borderline psychopath, he's just not clever enough.

Is your cat a psychopath?

ABOUT THE AUTHOR
Purrfessor Tiddles graduated
from Feline University with a first in
Furrensic Creamanology.

Purrfessor Tiddles is an expert in all
things that happen in cat's little brains,
because they are one. It's a marvel how
they've managed to type up this study on
the psychology of cats using paws and an
old typewriter, but here we are.

Purrfessor Tiddles is currently working
deep undercover in a suburban house in
the UK taking notes on the family they
live with, researching for a new book on
how humans are all perverts.

Could Purrfessor Tiddles
be in your home? Judging you?

Acknowledgements

Dedicated to Humphrey
(the cat), the best cat anyone
could ever wish for.